The Whimsical World of Marion Wright – Revisited!

More Art and Stories
by Marion Wright

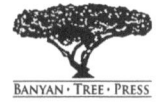

The Whimsical World of Marion Wright—Revisited!
More Art and Stories by Marion Wright
©2018 Marion Wright. All rights reserved.

No part of this publication may be reproduced or transmitted in any form or by any means, mechanical or electronic, including photocopying and recording, or by any information storage and retrieval system, without permission in writing from author or publisher (except by a reviewer, who may quote brief passages and/or show brief video clips in review):

ISBN: 978-1-948261-11-1

Cover Design and Interior Layout by: Ronda Taylor, HeartWork Publishing, www.heartworkpublishing.com

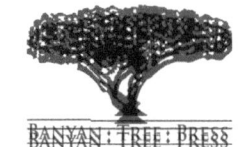

Austin, TX • Englewood, CO
www.BanyanTreePress.com

Dedication

This book is dedicated to my wonderful family and to all those I love so very much. All of you helped me with ideas that got me started on the paintings you will see in this book. My heart cannot express the gratitude I feel for what you have done! Just saying a word or a phrase to me often will give me an idea, and I rush downstairs to my studio where I grab a brush and begin painting. Thank you! Thank you! Thank you!

Marion Wright
Denver, Colorado 2018

Contents

Introduction vii
Burglar Scaring Machine 3
Cityscape With Fork In Road 4
The Cloud Processor 7
Dinosaur Washing Station 8
Fashions From the 16th Street Mall 11
The Girl Who Had a Level Head 12
The Long Way To Tip Arary 15
Martian Father And Son 16
Modern Man 19
Mother Goose's Robot 20
Neptunian Potentate And Lady 23
Porklift 24

Portrait Of An Airhead 27
Portrait Of Host-Anna Haf 28
The Prince Of Polaris And His Kwikeldrim 31
Round Tuit Processor 32
The Sheep To Sleep Machine 35
Two Friends From Pluto Enjoying A Snack 36
Udderly Ridiculous 39
Woman With Hat And Friends 40

Introduction

After I wrote the first book in 2011, friends started asking me when I was going to write another! It took a long time to make the paintings, but with the help of wonderful friends, we managed to publish, "*The Whimsical World of Marion Wright – Revisited!*"

I am extremely grateful to Dr. Patricia Ross and her team at Banyan Tree Press who worked so very hard to get this book out. My gratitude also extends to Matt Simmons of Catalyst Photo who did an outstanding job photographing my paintings. I so much appreciate my wonderful friends who encouraged me to write this book and who lent me their paintings to be published. I couldn't have done it without all of you and thank you over and over again!

I wish you peace and love!

Marion Wright
Denver, Colorado 2018

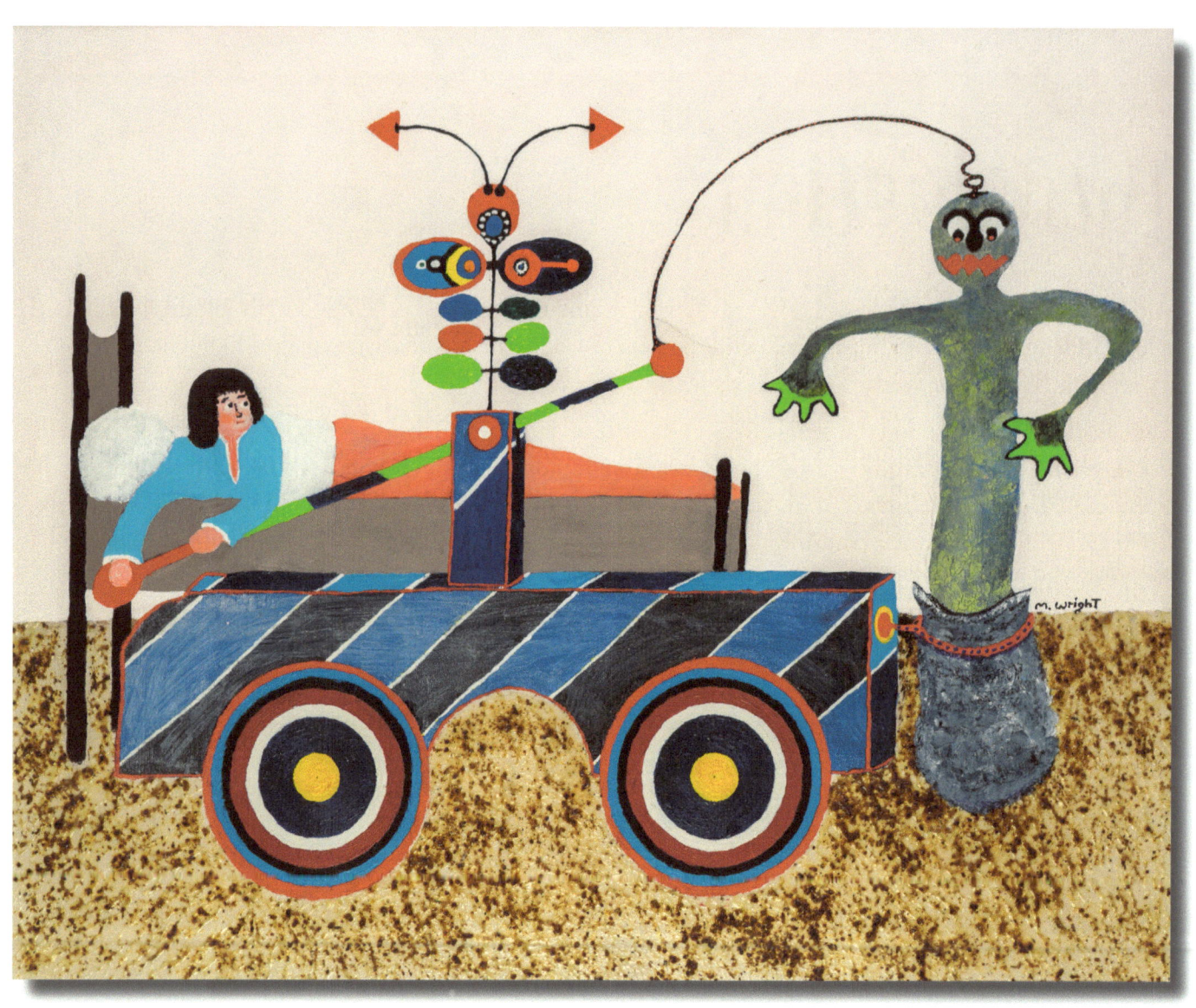

Acrylic on Canvas
24" x 30"
1984

Burglar Scaring Machine

If you live alone, you should consider getting one of these machines.

A burglar will prey on people who live by themselves because he has fewer chances of being caught in the act. He also usually will break into your house at night because he can get in and out under cover of darkness. As a result, you probably won't know he has been there until the next morning.

This machine is easy to use. Roll it up next to your bed and make sure the ghost made of green paper is stuffed into the plastic bag. When the burglar comes into your bedroom, press down on the lever to bring the ghost up. The sound of the paper ghost against the plastic bag will scare the burglar, and he will run away. We hope that in his fright he will drop all of your stolen possessions.

When you use this machine, no one gets hurt and the burglar leaves your house in a hurry. Through research we have learned that his world is small and most probably he has associates who are also burglars. It is hoped that he is so frightened by the ghost, that he tells his friends not to come to your place because it is haunted.

Cityscape With Fork In Road

A long time ago a friend and I went to Universal Studios in California where we saw an exhibit where all the buildings were fronts. The place looked like a city from the thirties, and there was even an old car parked on the street. We went up to the door of one of the buildings and, looking through a crack, noticed that the "building" was only three inches thick!

The buildings in this painting are like that, but less realistic. In some cases you can see the background through doors and holes in the buildings. I tried to give the painting a sense of mystery because the content is so unusual. Also, if you look closely, you can see that not all the buildings are lined up properly. It would certainly be interesting and different to live in one of these houses!

Finally, I decided to put a fork in the road. I reasoned that every street has a fork somewhere in it, so this street deserved one too!

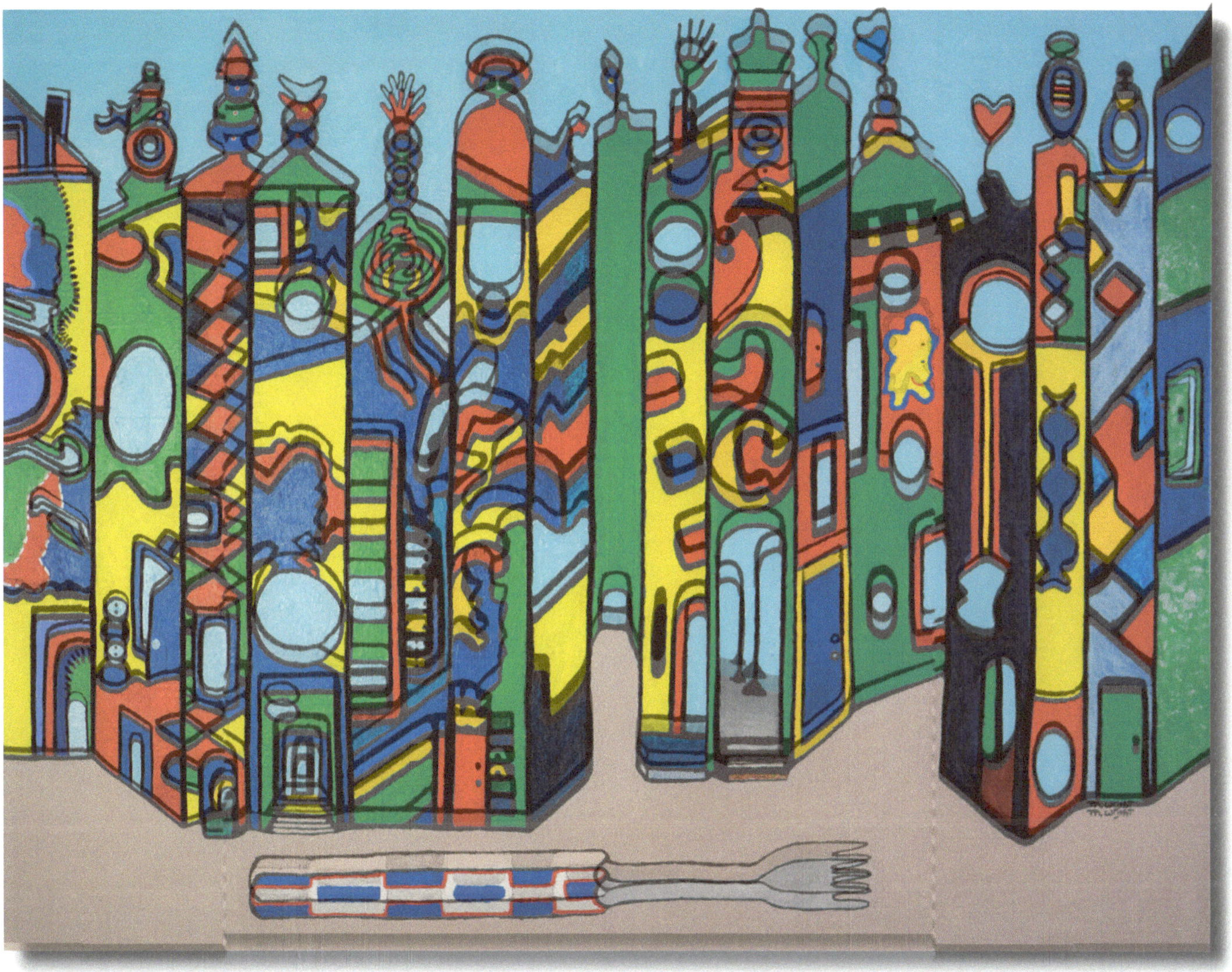

Acrylic on Canvas
30" x 40"
2016

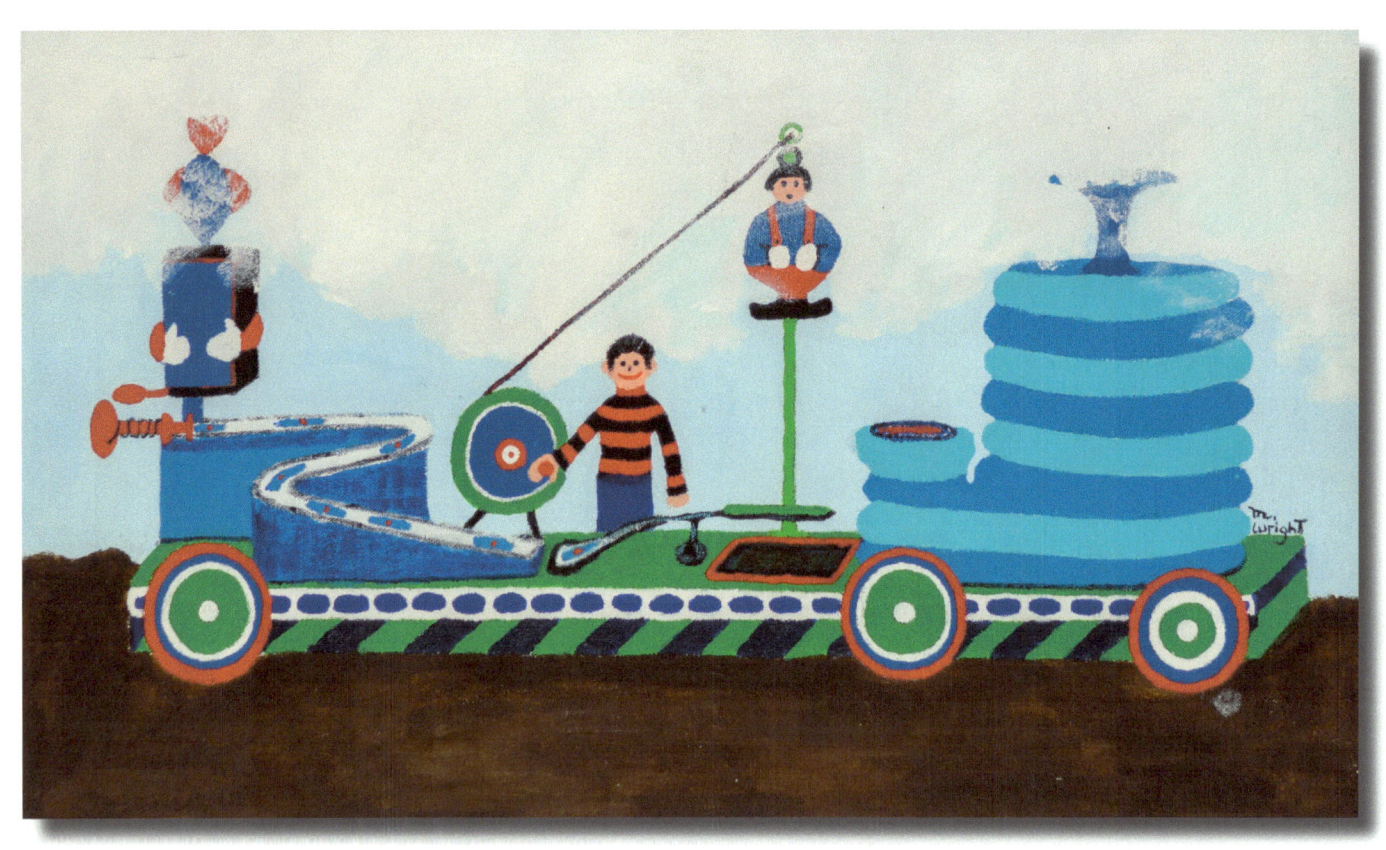

14" x 24"
Acrylic on Canvas
1990

The Cloud Processor

This machine is the only one of its kind in the world at this time. The unprocessed clouds are made in a controlled environment where they can be kept at the best temperature to function properly. Clouds are very delicate and will not form unless the conditions are right.

The unprocessed clouds (otherwise known as "cloudlets") are stored in the dark blue box with the white hands on the left side of the machine. Pull the red lever on the bottom of the box and the cloudlets will drop out one by one onto the ramp. The ramp is slippery, and the cloudlets should slide down easily to the second stage of their development. Pull the red knob with the spring to push the cloudlets if they do not move on their own. While they are on their way down the ramp, they are becoming acclimatized to the temperature and humidity of the environment.

When the cloudlets fall onto the lever in the middle of the machine, the operator turns the wheel which raises the heavy figure in red and blue. When the operator lets go of the wheel, the figure falls on the lever, and the unprocessed clouds are hurled into the machine.

After about twenty minutes, the first clouds come out of the stack and it takes about a hundred cloudlets for a cloud to be formed. You can expect a soaking rain after about forty minutes.

If necessary, and for an extra charge, cloudlets can be processed to produce thunder and lightning.

Dinosaur Washing Station

For millions of years dinosaurs wallowed in slimy pools and had to deal with itching and painful mites under their hides.

Fortunately, humans discovered their plight and dinosaurs are now coming to washing stations to be groomed with clean water and soap. As a result, they are feeling much better and are learning that regular washing is healthier than the old way in the pools.

This is one of the smaller dinosaurs. When humans wash Brontosaurus or Tyrannosaurus Rex, they use ladders from a firetruck and sometimes scaffolding to handle his great size.

Note that if treated with care and understanding, dinosaurs are gentle and easy to handle.

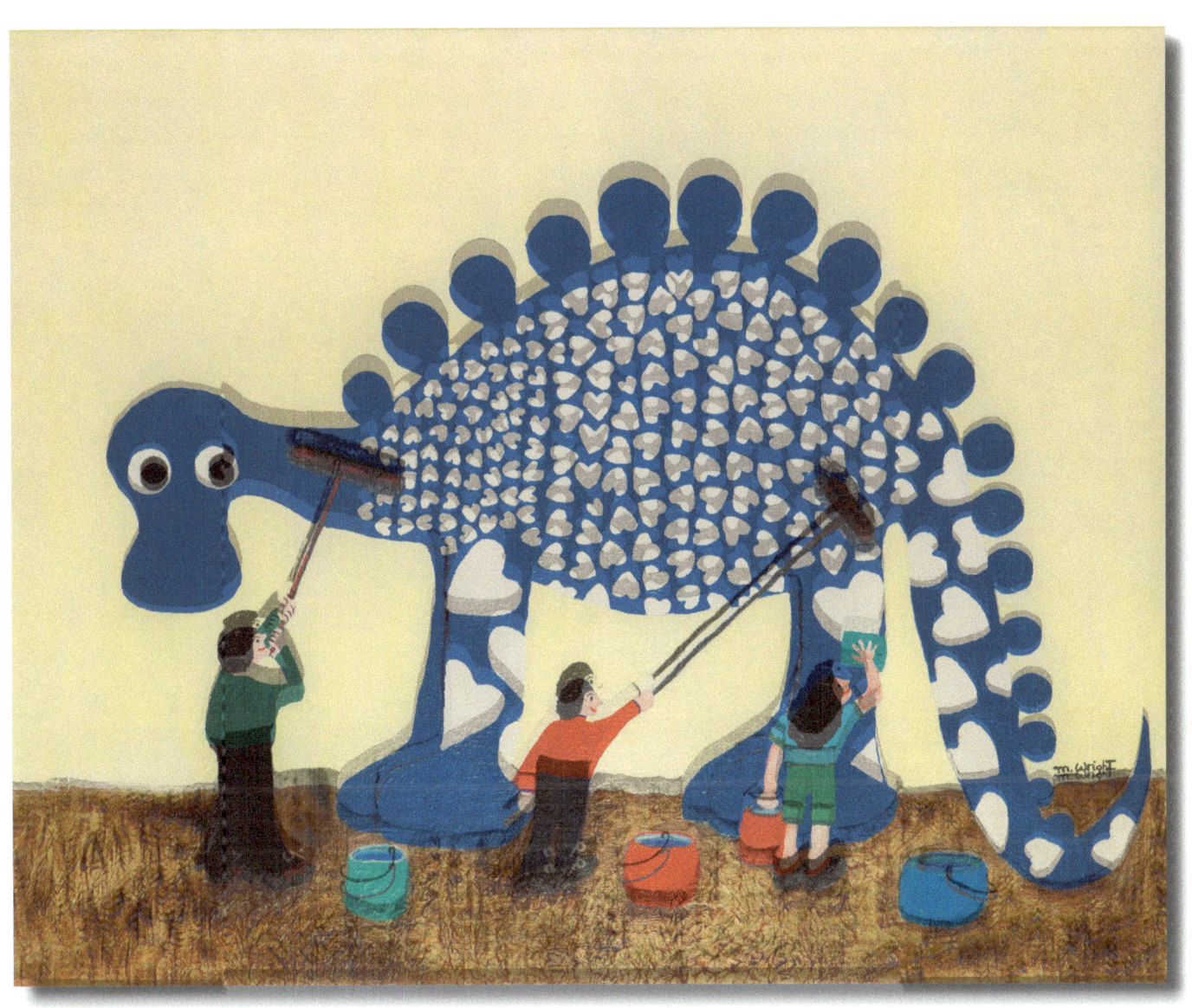

Acrylic on Canvas
24" x 30"
1989

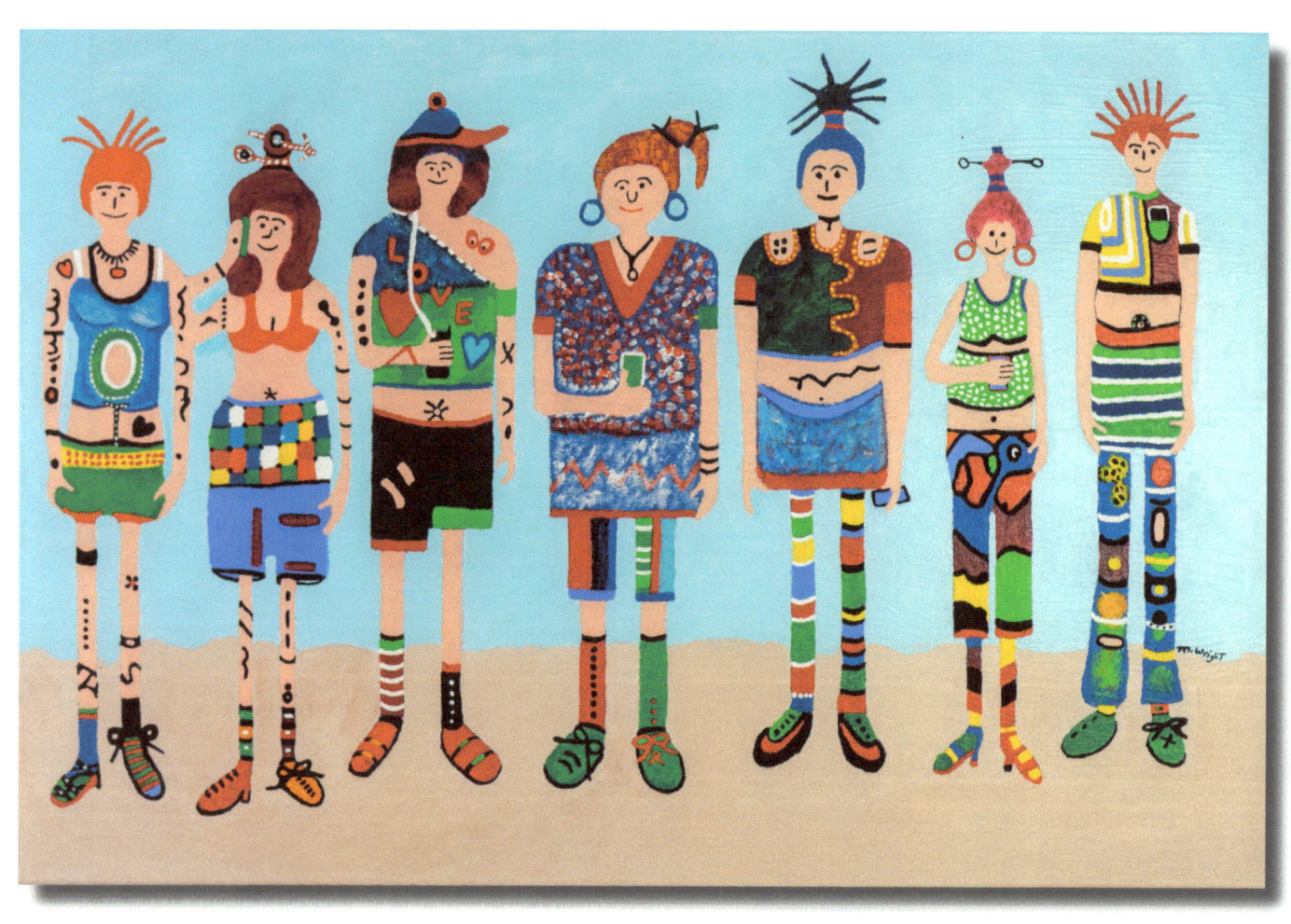

24" x 36"
Acrylic on Canvas
2018

Fashions From the 16th Street Mall

I have always been interested in people-watching, and a friend and I like to go to the 16th Street Mall. Once there, I sit unobtrusively on a bench and watch the "parade" going by. I rarely draw but I do take notes on what I see.

These seven figures are not actual copies, but composites of what has gone past me in an endless parade.

I have noticed that often our younger people do not interact, so I put my figures in a line looking straight ahead. All of them except the figure on the far left have cell phones that are visible, but she probably has one concealed somewhere.

Unusual hair styles and colors seem to be everywhere, so I enjoyed being creative with my brush. I wanted my seven figures to be up to the minute in their fashions.

This painting was a lot of fun to make.

The Girl Who Had a Level Head

This girl, whose name is Lucinda, has proved time after time that she does not get rattled or upset easily.

One day when there was a problem at school she calmly and efficiently led all her schoolmates out of the building. No one was hurt and she was credited for saving many lives.

At a later date during a special ceremony she was awarded a Certificate of Recognition from the School Board for her actions. However, her greatest joy was this fancy level which her classmates awarded her to be worn on her head.

She willingly posed for her portrait, wearing the level and her best dress.

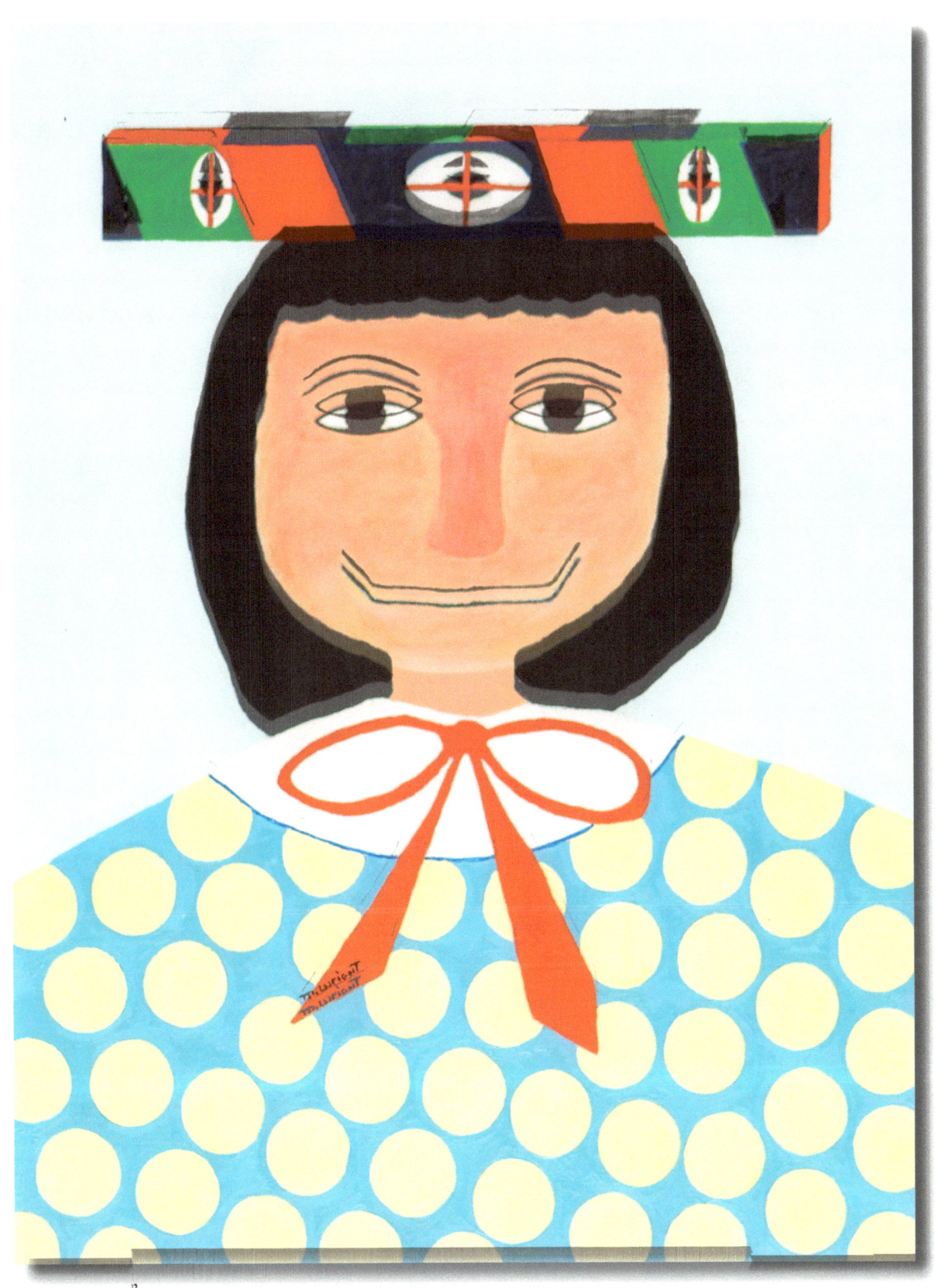

15" x 20"
Acrylic on Illustration Board
2002

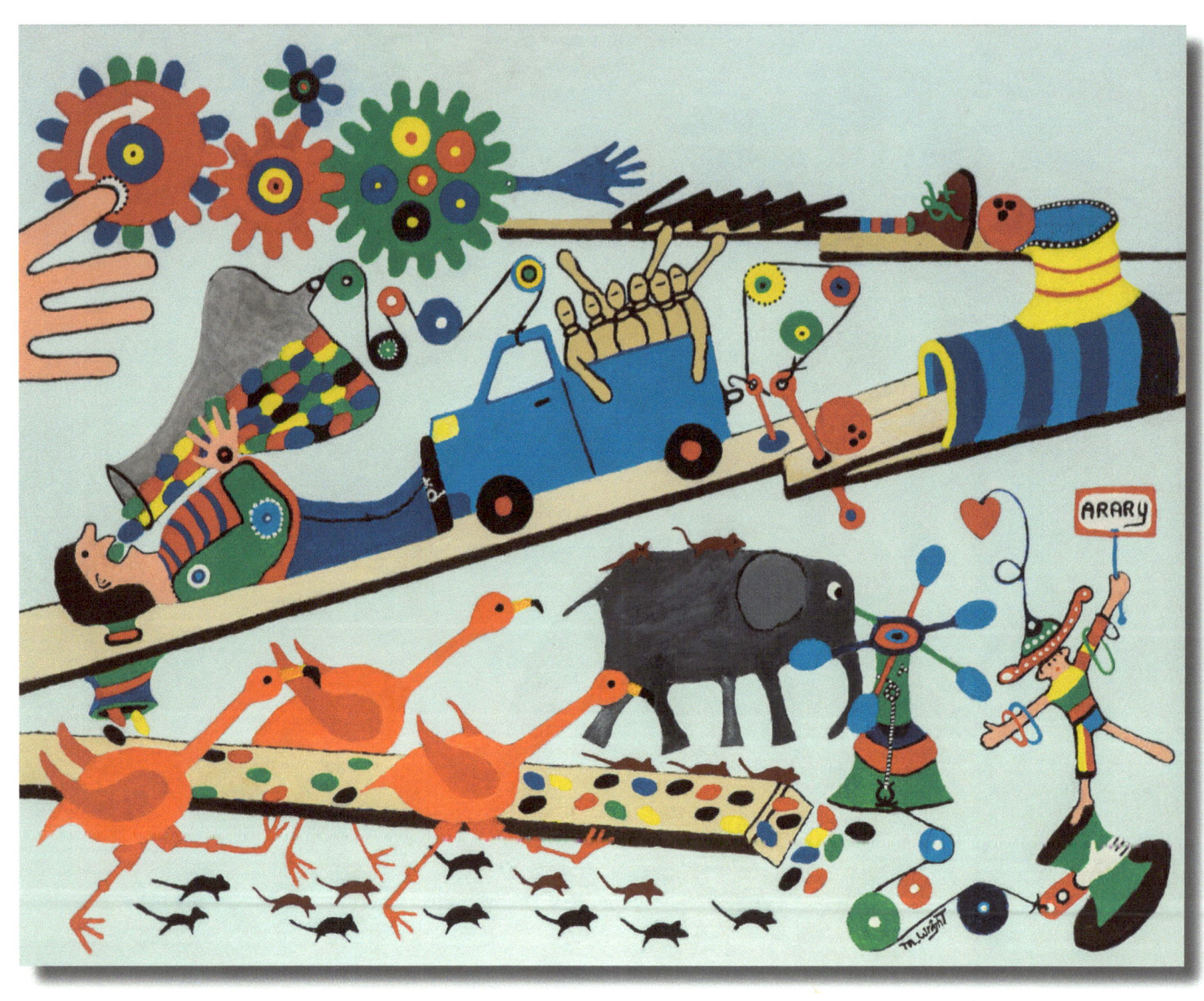

Acrylic on Canvas
22" x 28"
2016

The Long Way To Tip Arary

I have always been an admirer of Rube Goldberg, who designed machines made up of totally unrelated objects working together to perform a task at the end. This is a "Rube Goldberg" type machine.

This procedure starts at the upper left where you turn a gear which turns two other gears. The third gear has a hand on it which knocks over dominoes. The last domino has a boot on it which kicks the red bowling ball into a tube.

On the second level, the bowling ball exits the tube and hits the rod with a cable attached. When the rod moves, the cable is shortened and lifts the hook from the pickup truck. The released truck, carrying a load of artists' manikins, moves down the ramp and bumps into the feet of a robot.

A cable attached to the roof of the truck lifts the glass jar full of jelly beans, which fall into the mouth of the robot. The jelly beans go through the head of the robot and fall down on the ramp below.

Flamingo hens, believing that the jelly beans are their eggs, run along the ramp trying to get their "eggs" back. Frightened field mice run with them and jump on the back of an elephant.

The nervous elephant with mice on his back moves forward and turns the turnstile. This shortens the cable which pulls the white gloved hand down. The hand pulls the pedestal over and tips the character off. The name of the character is "Arary".

IT'S A LONG WAY TO TIP "ARARY"!

Martian Father And Son

Before attempting to paint this portrait, I studied Martian culture. Since they are reticent beings, I had to become acquainted with them to earn their trust. I also had to work in dim light as they are not accustomed to our intense sunlight.

The father, on the right, is the Grand Potentate of the planet as can be seen by his robe and elaborate scepter. His son is a prince and when his father dies he will become the next ruler. This royal family is very close and loving, and the son was happy to pose with his arm around his father.

Martians are able to hear and communicate by voice to those around them, and the antennae on their heads are used for long distance. They have only to think of the recipient in order to be in instant communication.

They are a gentle race of beings and are very curious about us. However, because of the long distance between us, it would be difficult for them to visit. We are hoping that sometime in the future we can meet them.

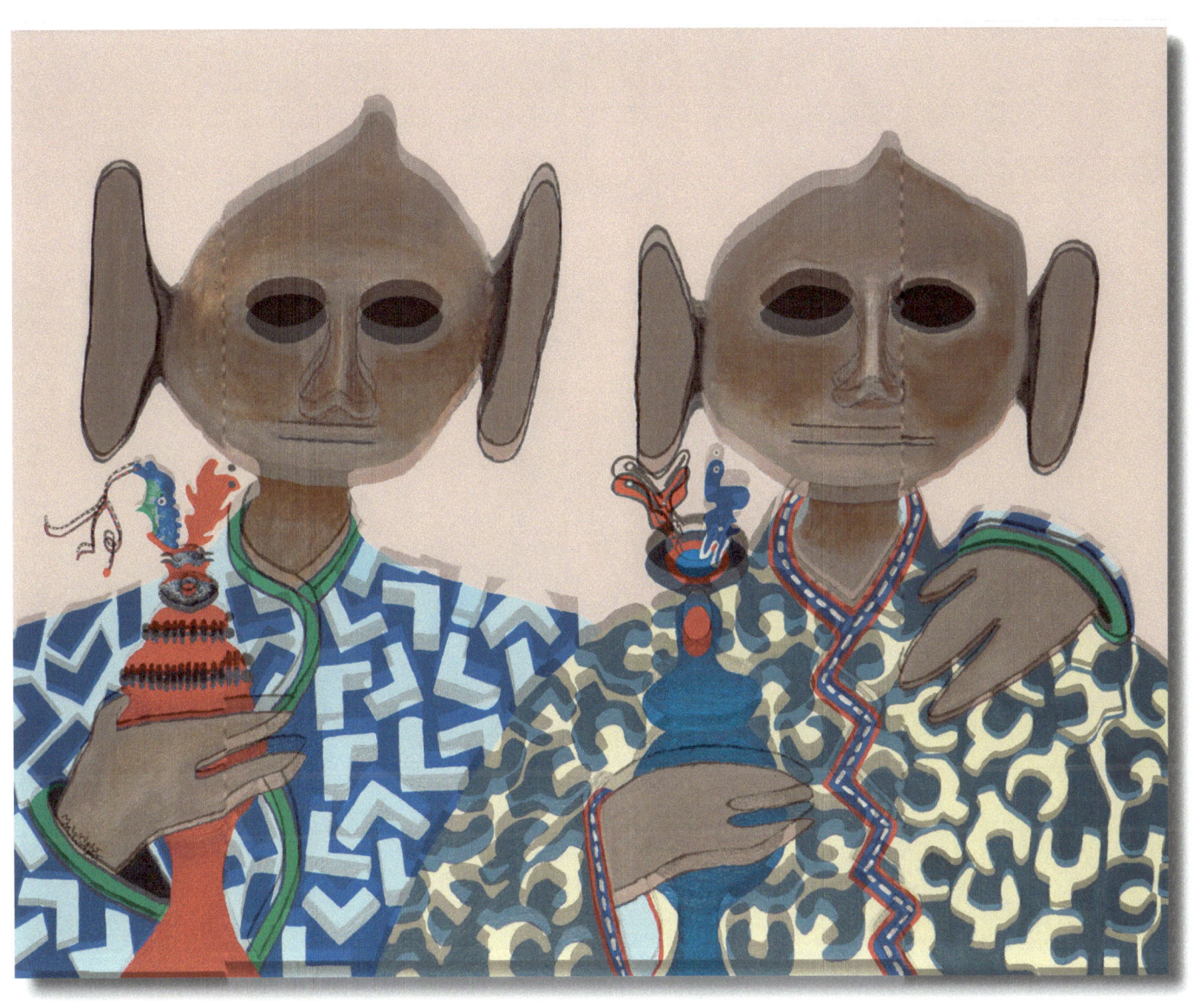

Acrylic on Illustration Board
20" x 30"
1994
With permission from the Adolf family of Denver

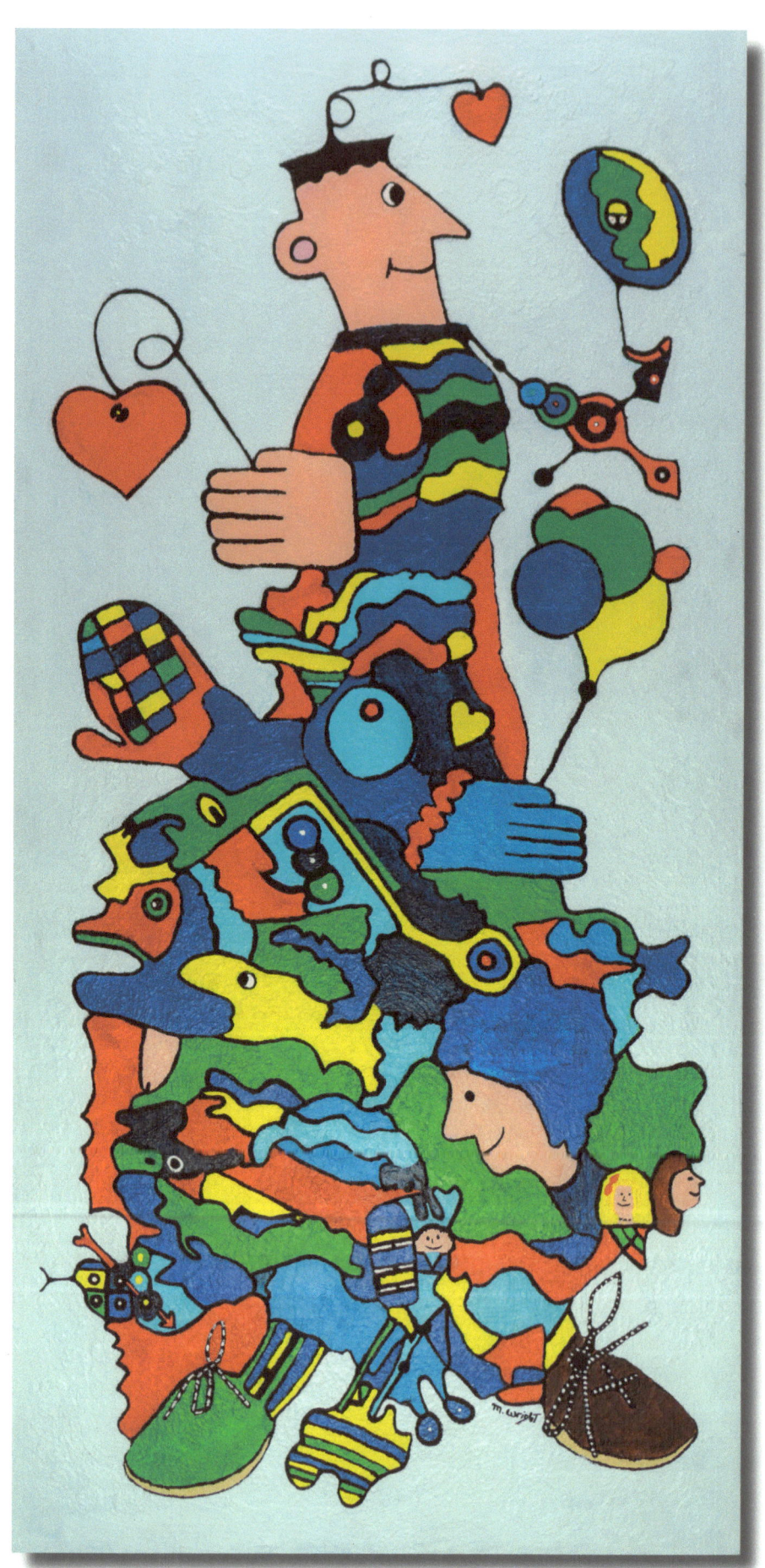

Acrylic on Canvas
24" x 48"
2016

Modern Man

This is a portrait of a modern man who is looking into a mirror where he sees a woman he once loved. Time has changed his memory of her and she is not quite complete, but he smiles when he thinks of her.

Meanwhile, he has a wife with blue hair and two daughters and a son whom he loves very much. We know also that he likes to grill, as there is a portrait of his favorite oven mitt on the left. For whatever reason, we see that he is wearing shoes of different styles and colors, and somewhere in his past he has a memory of a fish eating a duck.

One of the most fascinating features of humans is that we are complex individuals and all of us have memories!

Mother Goose's Robot
(2020 Model)

This is a portrait of Mother Goose test-driving the latest model of a robotic goose. Because of her job, she works all the time and she never knows when she will be asked to take a child or children for a ride.

Live geese take her flying whenever she needs to go, but they need their free time. They are on a schedule and need time off to raise their families and for vacations when they fly south. These times are in the contracts they set with her, and Mother Goose agrees that this is necessary. However, during the times the geese are off, she has to have transportation, so she flies a robot.

Robots, even those in the shape of a goose, need to be updated, and she is shown here flying the newest model: "The 2020 MG Goose-A-Rama". In this picture, Mother Goose is shown test-driving the model and taking children who are used to flying with her. Research has shown that pre-flown children are very relaxed and know how to respond to a mechanical goose.

This model is not out yet, but Mother Goose has been asked to test-fly it to be sure it has all the features she and her passengers need in order to be safe.

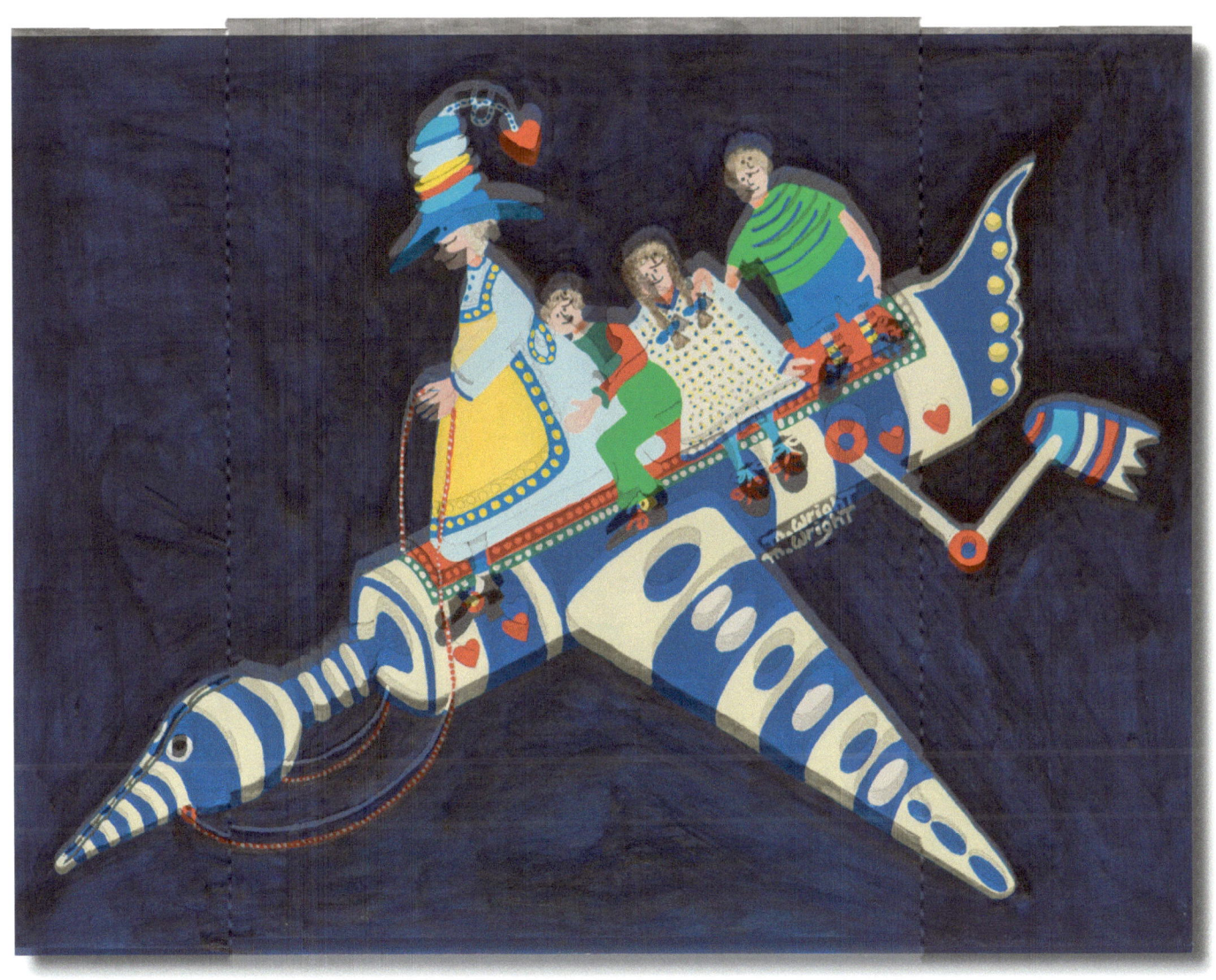

15" x 20"
Acrylic on Illustration Board
1998

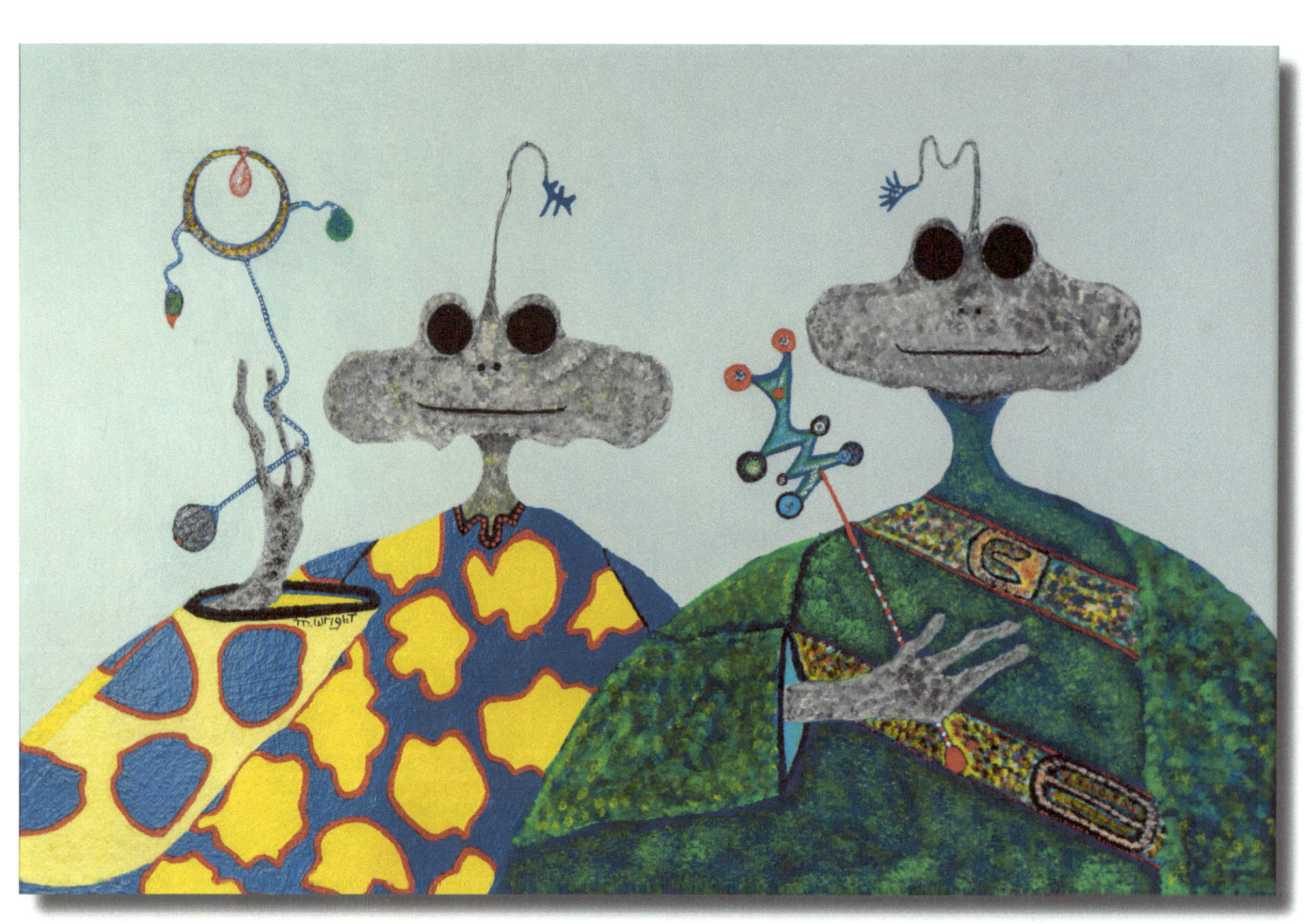

Acrylic on Illustration Board
25" x 35"
1995

Neptunian Potentate And Lady

This is a portrait of Neptunian royalty. The Potentate, on the right, is the ruler of the planet, and his Lady assists him. As is true in many monarchies, the oldest son will inherit the planet when his father dies.

At first, they were reluctant to have their portrait made because they had never seen a brush and paint before. It was difficult for me to see them in the dim light, so I asked if I could use a lantern. However, they explained that the extra light would injure their eyes. We compromised by using the light from a hundred Neptunian fireflies so I could see details more clearly.

Neptunians are humanoids, but because of long exposure to intense radiation, their skin is dark and has the texture of fur. They have no ears, so they communicate telepathically through the antenna on the top of their heads. Their eyes are large and dark because Neptune is so far from the sun that they do not have much light. Her Majesty does not carry her scepter very often because it is so light that it floats away if she lets go of it.

Though they look fierce, Neptunians are a gentle race and live their lives with love and kindness. When they heard we were sending a delegation to meet them, they were very excited about our visit.

I was so very pleased and complimented to be the first Earthling to make a portrait of beings from Neptune!

Porklift

If you are feeling down and out, you need to take a ride on Porklift! This flying pig will help you get rid of all your ills, and when you disembark you will feel much better!

Porklift is actually a robot partly inflated with Helium which makes him very light. He is controlled by sensors on the ground and there is always someone nearby to ensure that everyone on board is safe.

The chair swings back and forth as the machine moves through the air, soothing and calming those aboard. Those who have treated themselves to a ride have often said it was one of the most pleasant experiences they had ever had.

The next time you are at an amusement park, be sure to ask someone where Porklift is. I know you will enjoy your ride on this remarkable machine.

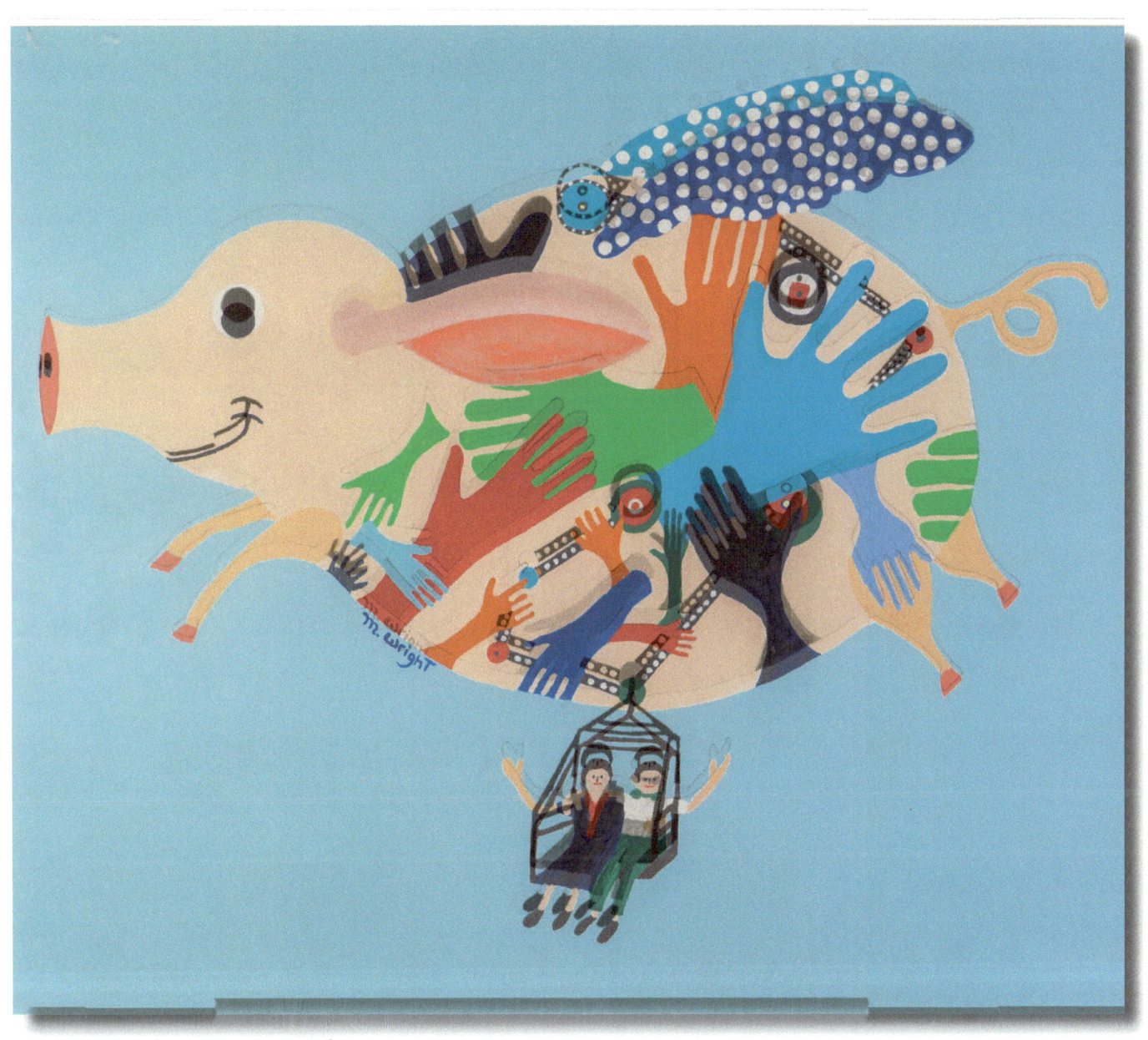

Acrylic on Illustration Board
20" x 30"
2001

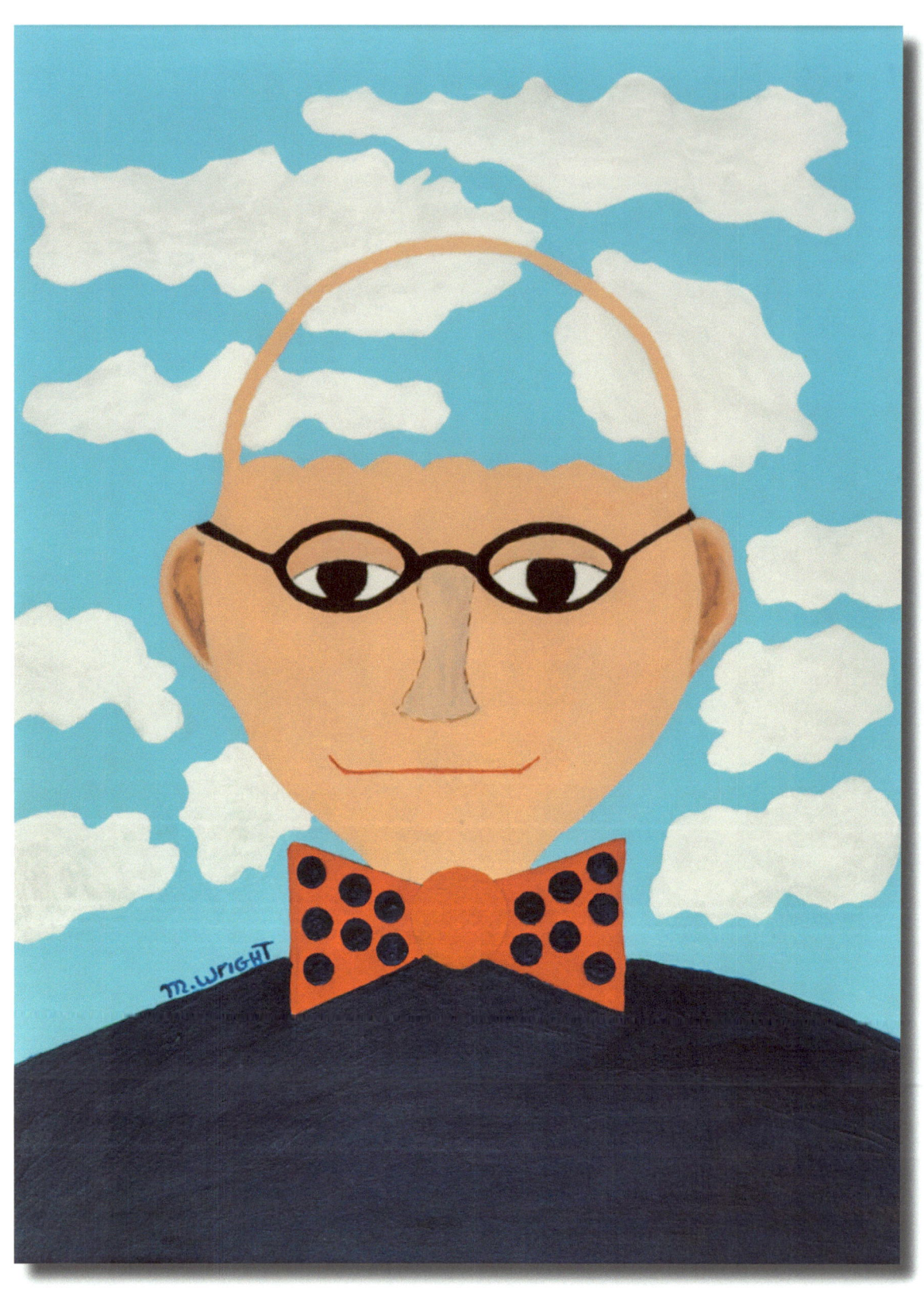

Acrylic on Illustration Board
15" x 20"
2001

Portrait Of An Airhead

This man, whom people giggle about and call an "airhead" is actually a genius. The difference is that his thoughts are in the clouds, and most people don't understand this concept. He thinks differently from everyone else, and his interests are considered to be "far out in left field".

For example, this brilliant man wonders about the metabolism of a paramecium and also the difference in hydrogen levels between the toes on the right foot from those on the left. Several years ago, he researched and wrote a report on "The Intrinsic Value of Vertical Asymptotes". This work was published and highly regarded by his colleagues, most of whom think the way he thinks.

Airheads are to be valued and not put down for their "way out ideas." From their brains have come inventions we could not live without today. Thomas Jefferson, Ben Franklin, Albert Einstein, Galileo, and The Wright Brothers were all airheads. If you know an airhead, give him or her a chance! They all helped to build our world and we would live totally different lives if it hadn't been for them!

Portrait Of Hoot-Anna Haf

Hoot-Anna Haf comes from a long line of milliners who are extremely proud of their ability to design and build unusual hats.

Hoot-Anna designed this one herself, using scraps from the floor as well as "found objects" from the street, and those given her by friends and associates. This is a very complex head covering, and most certainly there will never be another like it! No one is sure where or when she will wear it, but without question it will end up in her vast hat collection.

This painting sat on my easel for several months while I tried to give it a name. I showed it to friends who suggested "Woman in Hat" and "Wing-Ding Woman" among other names, but none of them seemed to be appropriate.

Then one day friends came to a party at my house and noticed this painting in my living room. While standing in front of the easel, one said to the other, "Isn't she a hoot and a half?!" I knew at that time that this portrait had to be named Hoot-Anna Haf.

This was a lot of fun to paint because I was able to make it as ridiculous as I wanted. I hope you enjoy it as much as I did while I was making it.

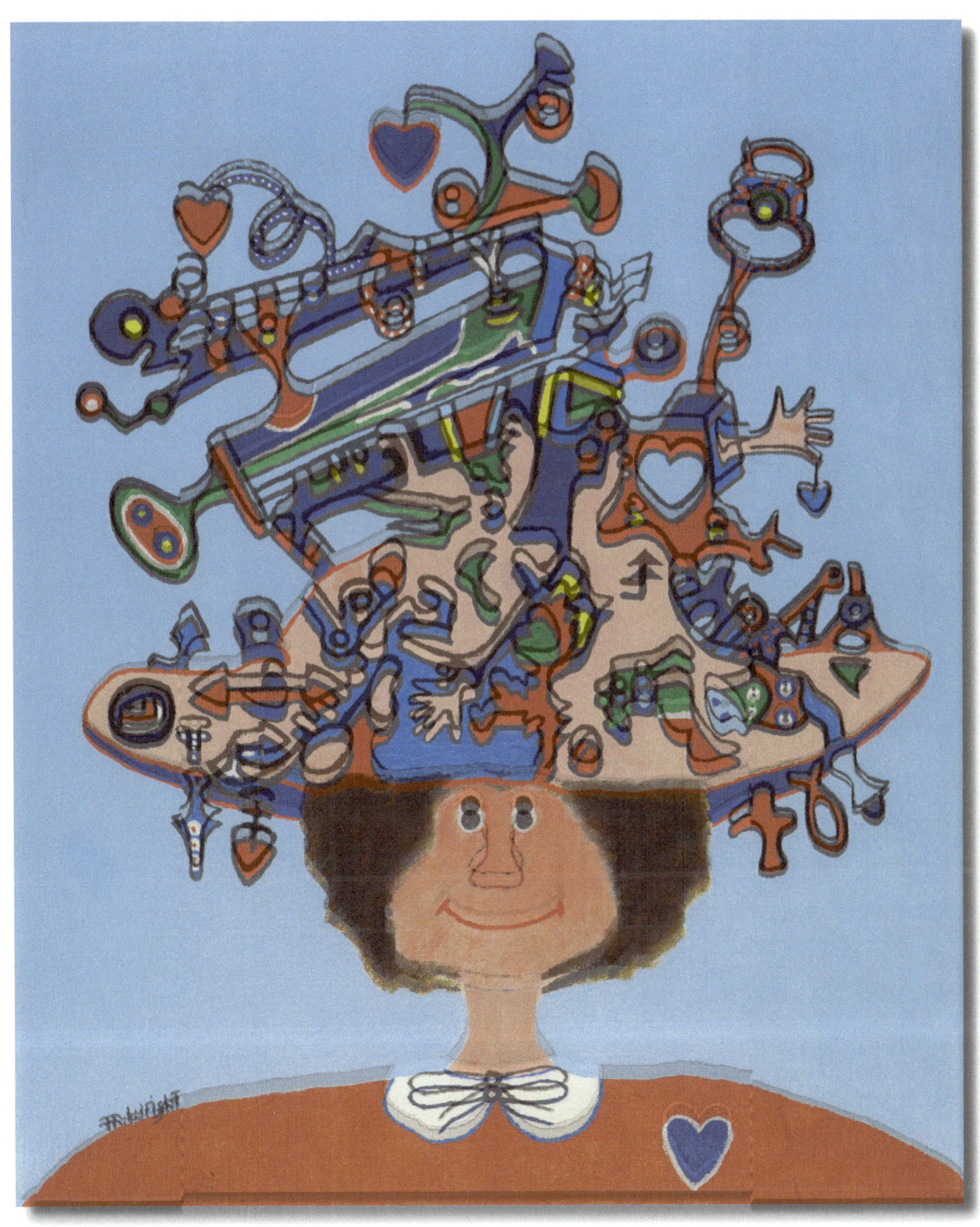

Acrylic on Canvas
20" x 24"
2018

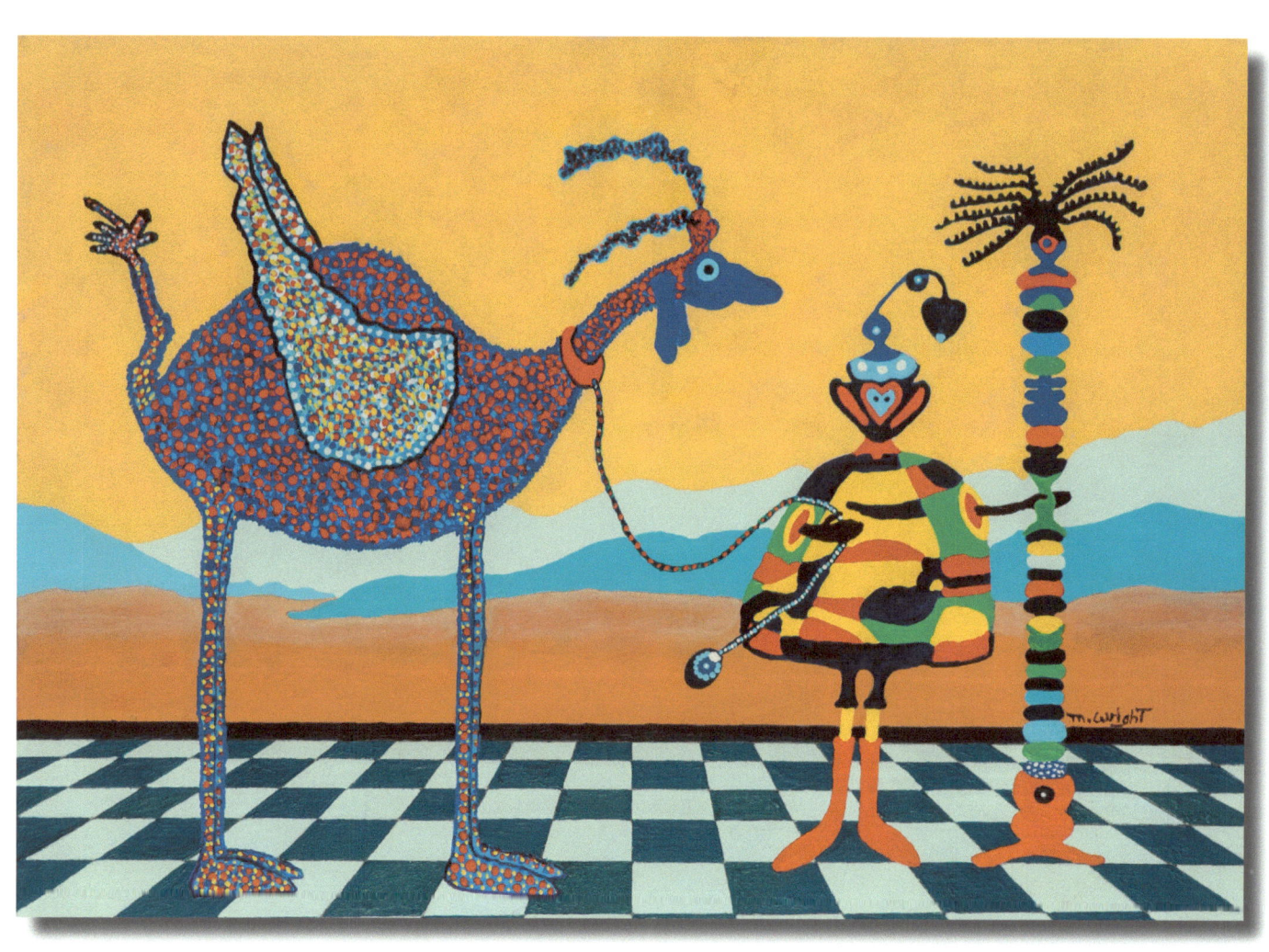

Acrylic on Illustration Board
15" x 20"
1986

The Prince Of Polaris And His Kwikeldrim

This portrait was painted on the veranda of the palace of the Royal Family of Polaris. Polarians are shy, and it was difficult to get anyone to pose, but the son of the King agreed to do it as long as he could be with his kwikeldrim. This young man is in royal garb, and he is seen with a tall and colorful scepter which denotes his status.

The kwikeldrim looks like a camel that can fly, but it is an animal totally unique to Polaris. For thousands of centuries, princes of this planet have had them as pets. The kwikeldrim is a gentle animal, easy to raise and train. Although they cannot be ridden, they are treated like family members and are often seen roaming through the Royal palaces.

It was evident that the Prince and his pet had a close association.

Round Tuit Processor

Have you ever wished you could get a round tuit? If so, this machine is the answer to your problems!

Tuits are manufactured in the shape of bricks and are loaded into the processor through the large funnel on the left. While inside the machine they go through three stages and come out of the stack on the right. They are round and very hot when they first exit the machine, so they need to be caught in nets.

It is imperative that tuits are caught as soon as possible after they leave the processor. If they fall on the ground or are allowed to grow cold before being caught, they are useless and must be sent back to the factory.

Once you have caught a tuit, it is yours and you cannot exchange it or trade with anyone else. For best effect, a tuit needs to be used as soon as possible.

If someone asks you if you have done what you said you were going to do, you can tell them that you finally were able to get a round tuit.

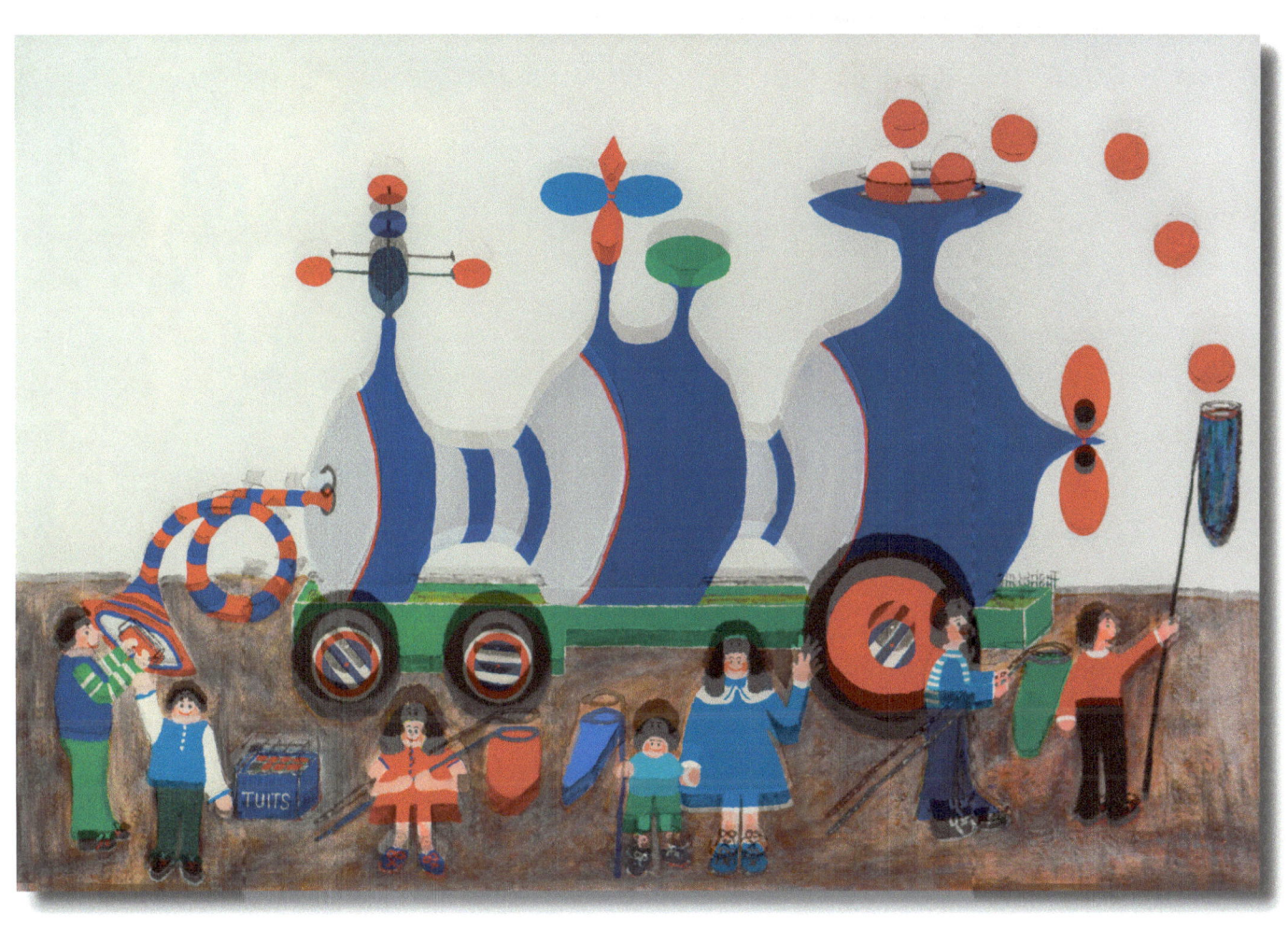

Acrylic on Canvas
24" x 36"
1988
With permission of the Adolf family, Denver, Colorado

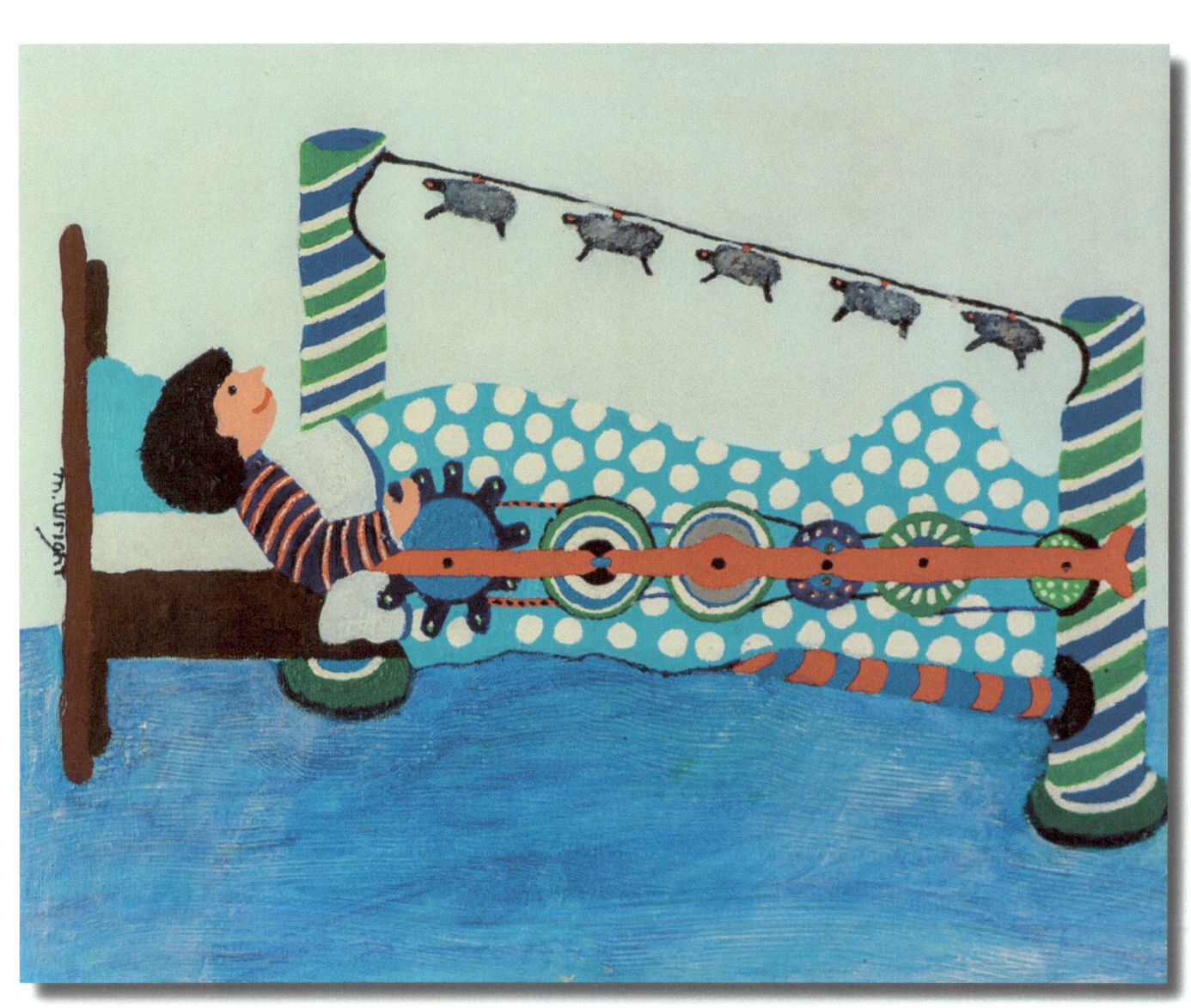

Acrylic on Canvas
16" x 28"
By permission of the Buznedo family

The Sheep To Sleep Machine

Have you ever been bothered by insomnia? You toss and turn and cannot get to sleep. Counting sheep doesn't help and neither does the new pillow you purchased the day before.

This machine will help you go to sleep instantly. It fits over any size bed and is simple to use. You turn the crank on the side of the machine and count the sheep leaping over your bed. After going over your head they go down a tube, go under the bed, and reappear from the tube at the bottom of your bed. As long as you keep cranking, the sheep will continue to jump over your head.

Eventually you will go to sleep either from boredom or from exhaustion from turning the crank all night. This machine works every time!

Two Friends From Pluto Enjoying A Snack

This is a portrait of Plutonian friends sharing a meal. It is very difficult to grow food on Pluto as it is almost all rock without much moisture. As a result, they cannot produce much vegetation so they grow their food in the bags you see here.

These bags are specially made so any available moisture can be stored and put to use. In this case the being on the left has unplugged the bag and squeezed it to push out the meal, which he is sharing with his friend. He will put the cap on the bag immediately so the food will not dry out. The organisms in the bag will multiply within an hour and more food will be created within two hours. These two have been friends all their lives and willingly share their meal.

Plutonians have very thin, elongated heads, and their hands are shaped like mittens. They wear long robes and head gear for protection from the elements, but after two hundred generations of exposure to intense radiation, these mutations have occurred.

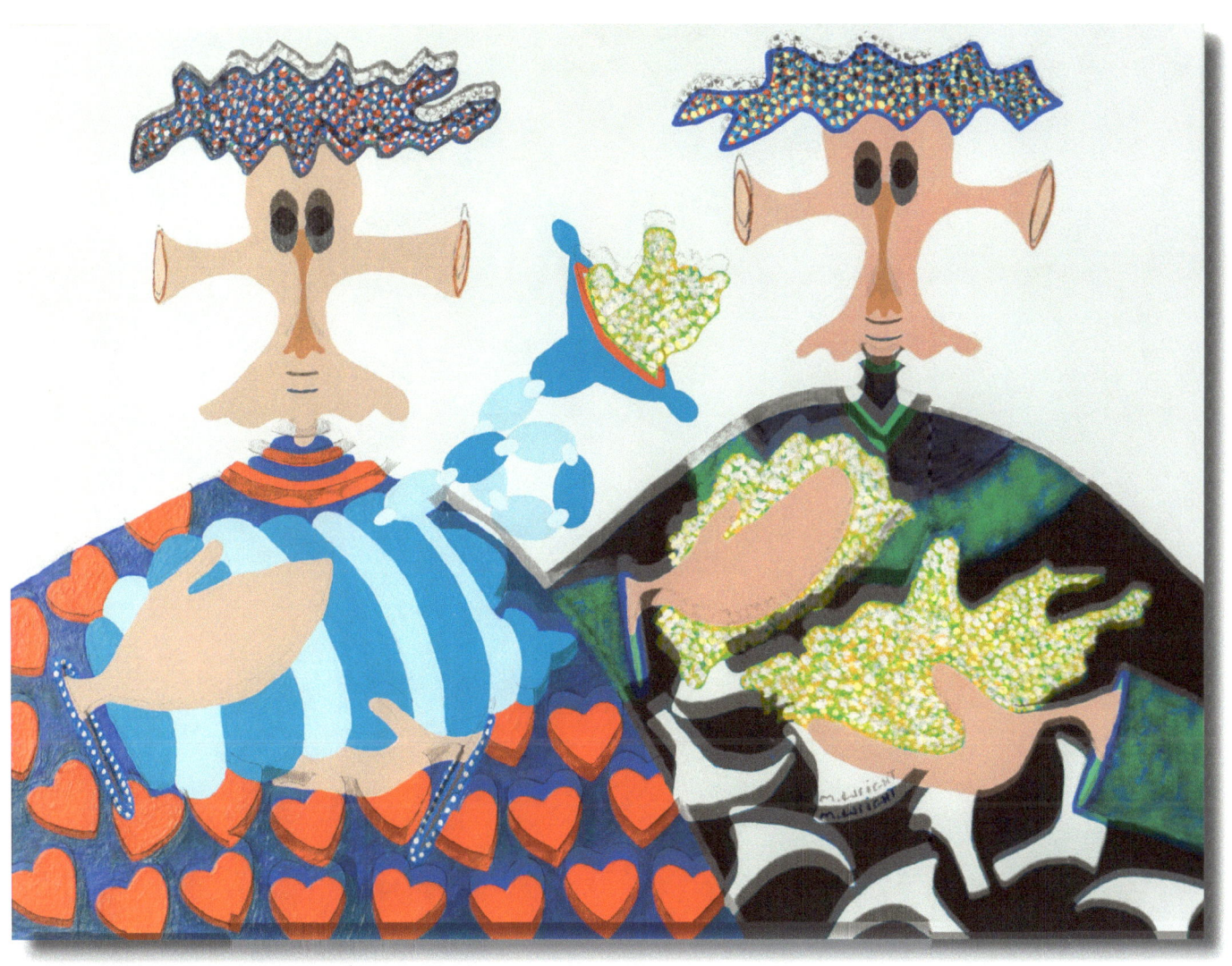

Acrylic on Illustration Board
15" x 20"
1996

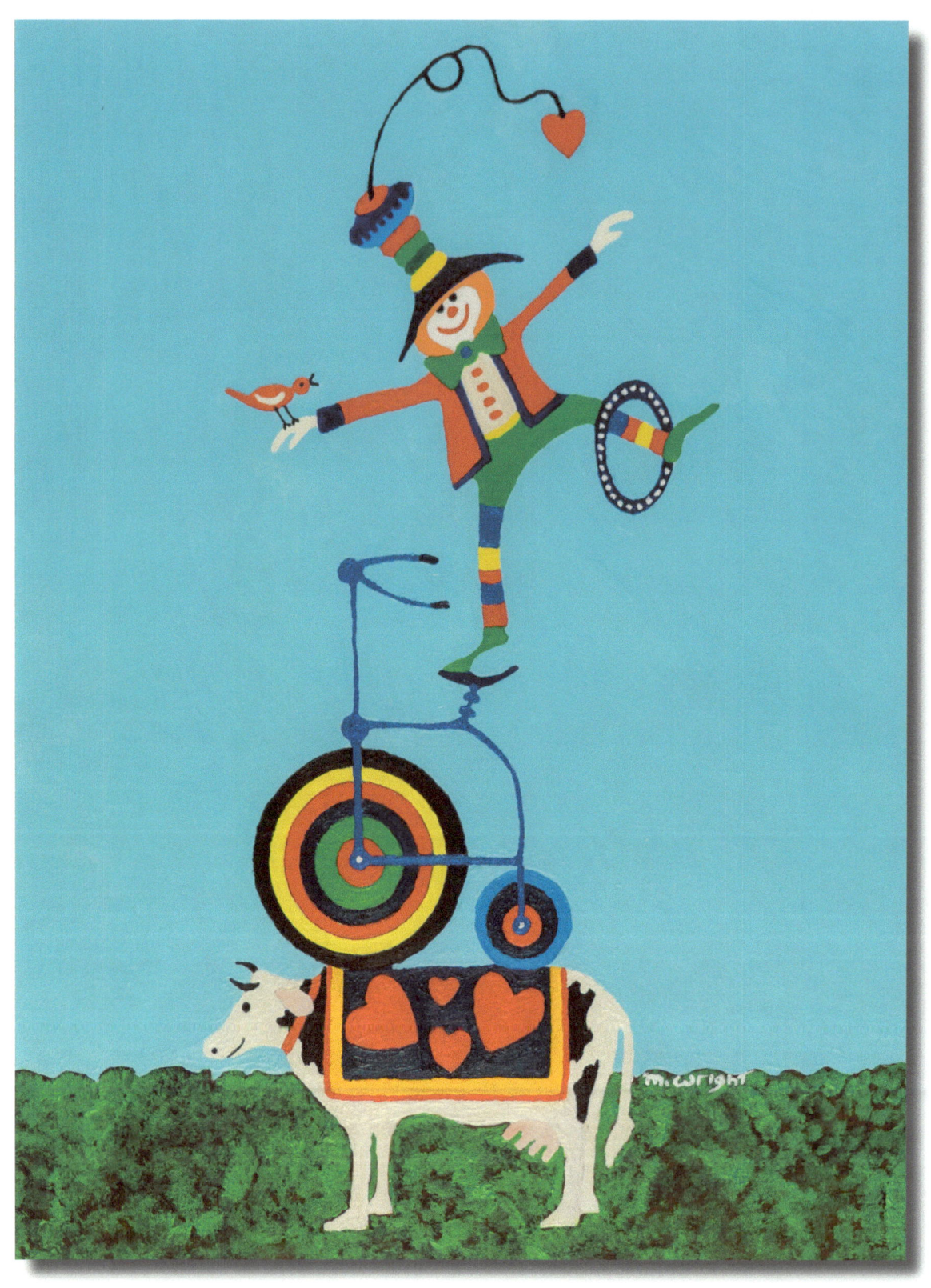

15" x 20"
Acrylic on Illustration Board
2005

Udderly Ridiculous

This clown is performing an act that many would think is impossible to do! Juggling with your foot while standing on a bicycle on the back of a cow would be a serious balancing act with a lot of concentration! First you would have to learn to juggle, and then stand on your toe on the seat of a bicycle on the back of a cow. Most important of all, you would have to train your cow to stand still so you could do your act while your pet bird sits on your hand!

Training a cow to stand absolutely still would be very difficult and would take a long time. Cows know what to do to survive, such as eating grass and hay, having a calf and giving milk. Standing still while you put a bicycle on her back would be hard for her to understand, and you would have to be very patient. One toss of her head or flick of her tail and the act would be ruined.

It seems to me these two have been working together for a long time, and they understand each other very well.

This painting was fun to do, but I think my brush took over!

Woman With Hat And Friends

This is a portrait of relationships. The woman on the left wearing the hat is unaware that the two others are admirers. She knows the second woman but passes her off as an acquaintance. However, the second woman thinks the woman wearing the hat is her good friend.

As for the man with the buck teeth, he holds the two women in high regard, but he is too shy to let them know how he feels. He believes that because his teeth are crooked and he has an eye problem, others will think he is stupid. Therefore, he stays in the background and the women will never have a chance to know how nice he is.

These three have issues which are preventing them from enjoying relationships with others. The woman with the hat does not care about anyone else and relates only with those who show interest in her. The second woman fails to realize what is going on with the first woman and keeps trying to improve the relationship. The first woman is self-centered and cares little for the second woman, so that relationship will never go anywhere. As for the man, he will stay in the background all his life, believing that no one will ever care about him because he is dumb and ugly.

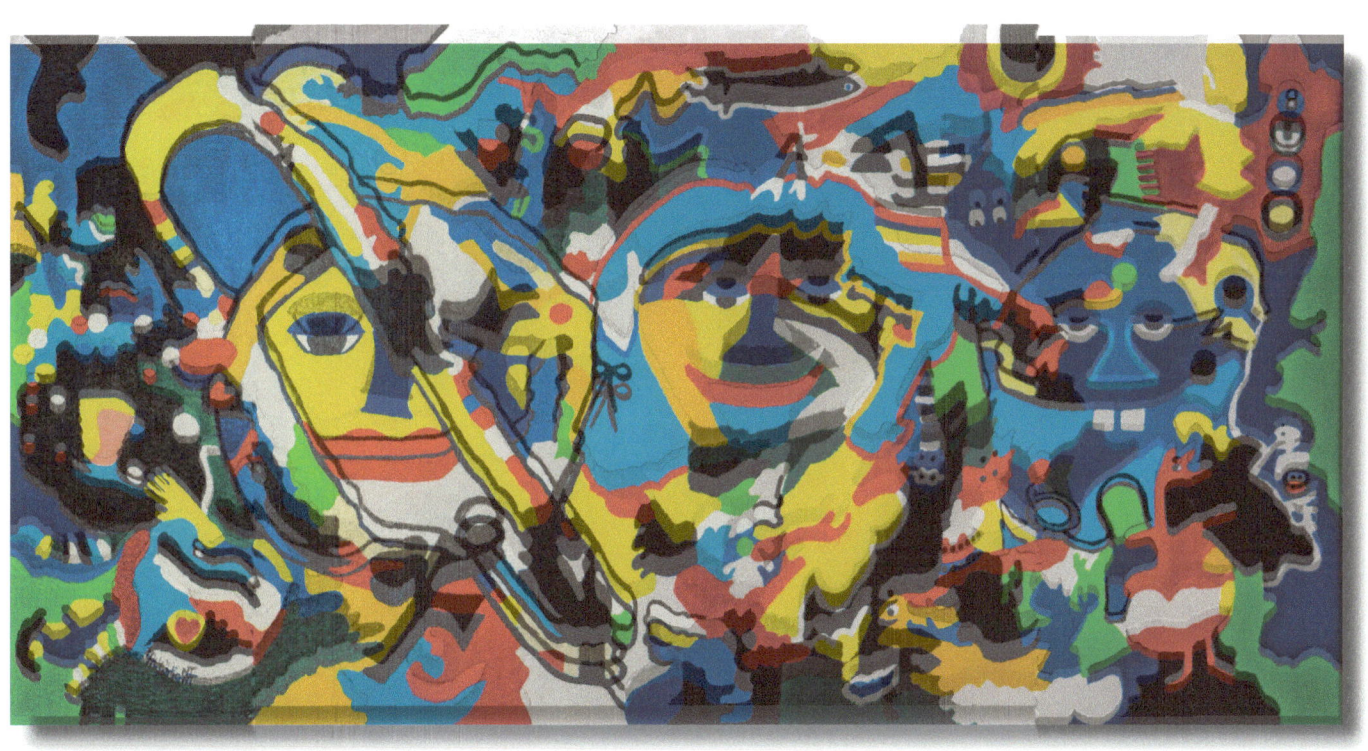

Acrylic on Canvas
18" x 36"
2009

About the Author

Marion Wright was born and grew up in Washington, D.C. except for two years in England and eight years in Virginia. She moved to Denver in 1974 and has made that her home. She went to Metropolitan State College in Denver and majored in fine art with a specialty in painting. She has sold work in Denver, Omaha, Washington, D.C. and Edinburgh, Scotland. When not painting, Marion likes reading, music, photography, travel, and spending time with friends and loved ones.